SUMMIT PUBLISHING

Arctic Canines Unleashed

A Handbook of Five Majestic Breeds

This book was professionally typeset on Reedsy.
Find out more at reedsy.com

Contents

1

Introduction

Welcome to the Arctic Wilderness

Prepare to embrace a world where the air is brisk, the snow blankets the landscape in a brilliant white tapestry, and the cold winds carry the echoes of a distant past. This unforgiving place at the top of the world is the Arctic Wilderness, a realm where nature reigns supreme, and survival is an art form. We're thrilled to be your guide on this exhilarating journey into the heart of the Arctic and the captivating world of Arctic canines.

Definition and Characteristics of Arctic Breeds

A group of remarkable canine companions thrives in the heart of the Arctic wilderness, painting this world in serene hues of ice and snow. These magnificent dogs, collectively known as Arctic breeds, embody the very essence of resilience, adaptability, and the untamed spirit of the North. Draped in thick fur coats, they possess striking appearances that have stirred the imagination for generations. As we embark on this gripping expedition to explore the realm of Arctic breeds, we must first define what sets these extraordinary canines apart and grasp the defining traits that render them the remarkable companions they genuinely are.

Arctic canines encompass a diverse ensemble of dog breeds; each uniquely adapted to flourish in the unforgiving conditions of the Arctic and sub-Arctic regions. These breeds share a common thread of characteristics that distinguish them amidst the rich tapestry of the canine world. Chief among these traits is their thick double coat, a natural marvel engineered by evolution to provide insulation against the Arctic's biting cold. This dual-layered coat is a protective shield against harsh elements and an invaluable source of warmth during the unforgiving winters.

However, the exceptionalism of Arctic breeds extends beyond the realm of physical attributes. These dogs possess an innate temperament and behavior as distinctive as their appearance. Renowned for their intelligence, independence, and unwavering work ethic honed through generations of adaptation to their challenging environment, they have cultivated an extraordinary ability to problem-solve, adapt, and thrive in the face of adversity—a testament to their remarkable nature.

Importance of Understanding Arctic Breeds

Understanding these cold-weather canines is not merely a pursuit of biological and behavioral knowledge; it is a profound exploration of the enduring bond between humans and animals—a testament to the remarkable connection forged in the crucible of the Arctic wilderness. It is a journey into the heart of our shared history, where these dogs have played pivotal roles in the survival, prosperity, and exploration of indigenous cultures, daring adventurers, and modern enthusiasts alike.

Arctic breeds represent more than just companions; they are living relics of a time when humans first sought the loyalty and assistance of these noble creatures in their relentless pursuit of survival. Their history is intertwined with ours, as they have served as essential partners in hunting, transportation, and companionship for the indigenous peoples of the North. These dogs have pulled sleds through unforgiving blizzards, tracked prey across the boundless tundras, and provided the warmth of their companionship during the darkest of Arctic nights.

Today, as we celebrate these fantastic canines' companionship and unwavering loyalty, we must acknowledge the depth of their heritage and the roles they continue to play in our lives. Whether they are cherished as beloved family members, working alongside search and rescue teams in treacherous conditions, or igniting the thrill of dog sledding races, these dogs epitomize the enduring power of the human-canine connection.

Overview of the Five Featured Breeds

As we embark on this enthralling expedition into the world of Arctic canines, five of this extraordinary group's most iconic and beloved representatives will accompany us. Each breed bears a unique narrative to share, a rich history to uncover, and a distinctive set of characteristics that set them apart within the realm of canines.

Our journey shall commence by introducing you to the Siberian Husky, whose history is deeply rooted in the Chukchi people and whose striking appearance is only rivaled by its friendly temperament and adaptability. We shall immerse ourselves in the majesty of the Alaskan Malamute, renowned for its strength and endurance, with a heritage tracing back to the Inuit tribes of Alaska. The Samoyed, celebrated for its gentle disposition and striking appearance, shall enchant us as we explore its history alongside the nomadic Samoyedic peoples.

From there, we shall venture into the world of the Greenland Dog, distinguished by its resilience and unique adaptations to the Arctic, leading us into the realm of working dogs in the icy expanses of Greenland. Lastly, we shall uncover the legacy of the Canadian Eskimo Dog, whose indigenous heritage and traditional roles intertwine deeply with the Arctic way of life.

This handbook delves deeper into these canines' lives, histories, and unique attributes. You will surely gain a profound appreciation for the remarkable connection between humans and dogs. This connection transcends time and embodies the very spirit of the North. Together, let us embark on this captivating exploration into the world of Arctic breeds, where loyalty, resilience, and the indomitable spirit of the North reign supreme.

2

Siberian Husky

H istorical Background and Origin

In the vast, frozen expanses of the Arctic, where the land meets the sky in a blur of white, a breed of dog thrives with a history as storied as the northern lights dancing above. The Siberian Husky, a breed known for its striking appearance and unwavering loyalty, is a testament to the resilience and adaptability required to survive in one of the harshest environments on Earth.

The Siberian Husky's origins can be traced back to the indigenous

Chukchi people of Siberia, who inhabited the inhospitable regions of the Russian Far East for centuries. These resourceful people relied on these dogs for companionship and as essential partners in their daily lives. The Chukchi people bred Huskies for their endurance, strength, and ability to navigate treacherous terrain. These canines were integral to their survival, pulling sleds loaded with supplies across vast frozen landscapes and assisting in hunting expeditions.

The rest of the world was introduced to the Siberian Husky in the early 20th century. During the 1925 Nome Serum Run, a life-saving mission to deliver diphtheria antitoxin serum to Nome, Alaska, Siberian Huskies played a pivotal role. They were among the heroic dogsled teams that braved extreme weather conditions and treacherous terrain to deliver the serum, saving countless lives and forever endearing themselves to the world.

Physical Characteristics

The Siberian Husky is renowned for its distinctive appearance, which combines beauty and functionality in perfect harmony. Their medium-sized bodies are well-muscled and compact, designed for endurance and agility. Their double coat, comprised of a soft, insulating undercoat and a straight, coarse outer coat, protects them against the bitter cold of the Arctic. This coat comes in various colors and markings, including black, gray, red, and agouti, often with striking facial masks and captivating blue eyes that brown or green hues can complement.

One of the most striking features of the Siberian Husky is its erect triangular ears, which exude an alert and intelligent demeanor. Along with their expressive almond-shaped eyes, their tails are plume-like and carried over their backs in a graceful arch. The overall appearance of the Siberian Husky is one of balance, grace, and strength.

Temperament and Behavior

While their captivating appearance may initially draw you in, the Siberian Husky's temperament and behavior truly endear them to those fortunate enough to share their lives. Huskies are known for their friendly and outgoing nature, making them excellent companions for families and individuals. They are affectionate, gentle, and warm-hearted, often forming strong bonds with their human counterparts.

However, it's essential to understand that the Siberian Husky possesses an independent streak, a characteristic honed through generations of working in the challenging Arctic environment. This independence can sometimes translate into stubbornness, requiring a patient and consistent approach to training. Huskies are intelligent dogs and thrive on mental stimulation. Engaging them in activities that challenge their minds, such as obedience training and puzzle toys, can help satisfy their mental exercise needs.

Their strong work ethic is another defining trait of Siberian Huskies. They have a natural desire to pull, which is a remnant of their sled-pulling heritage. This trait can be harnessed in various ways, from participating in dog sledding or skijoring to simply enjoying vigorous walks and runs with their human companions.

Training and Socialization

Training a Siberian Husky can be a rewarding experience, but it's essential to approach it with patience and consistency. Due to their independent nature, Huskies may only sometimes be eager to please.

Still, they can become well-behaved and obedient companions with positive reinforcement techniques and a firm yet gentle approach.

Early socialization is crucial for Huskies to ensure they become well-adjusted and confident dogs. Exposing them to various people, animals, and environments from a young age can help prevent shyness or aggression. Socialization also helps curb any tendencies towards stubbornness or assertiveness, making for a more harmonious relationship between the dog and its human family.

Health Considerations

Siberian Huskies are generally healthy, with a life expectancy of around 12 to 15 years. However, like all breeds, they are susceptible to specific health issues. One common concern is hip dysplasia, a genetic condition that affects the hip joints and can lead to arthritis and pain. Regular veterinary check-ups and responsible breeding practices can help mitigate the risk of hip dysplasia.

Another condition to be aware of is cataracts, which can develop in Huskies and potentially lead to vision impairment. Eye examinations by a veterinary ophthalmologist can help monitor and manage this condition.

Siberian Huskies are also prone to allergies and skin conditions, so keeping their coats clean and well-groomed is essential. Regular brushing can help remove loose hair and reduce shedding, which is more pronounced during seasonal changes.

Notable Siberian Husky Stories and Achievements

Throughout history, Siberian Huskies have left an indelible mark on our hearts and society. From their heroic role in the Nome Serum Run to their participation in modern dog sledding races, these dogs have repeatedly showcased their extraordinary capabilities.

One notable example is the story of Balto, a Siberian Husky who led his sled team through blizzards and sub-zero temperatures in 1925 to deliver the life-saving diphtheria antitoxin serum to Nome, Alaska. Balto's unwavering determination and resilience made him a symbol of heroism and courage, and a bronze statue in his honor stands proudly in New York City's Central Park.

Another Husky, Togo, played a crucial role in the same serum run, covering the journey's longest and most treacherous stretch. Togo's exceptional endurance and willingness to push through extreme conditions demonstrated the remarkable capabilities of the Siberian Husky.

Reaching further into the world of Arctic breeds will continue to uncover stories of bravery, loyalty, and the extraordinary bond between humans and dogs. The Siberian Husky's tale is one chapter in this captivating narrative, and our journey has only begun.

3

Alaskan Malamute

Origins and Cultural Significance

In the unforgiving landscapes of the Arctic and sub-Arctic regions, where the icy winds howl and snow blankets the earth for miles in every direction, another majestic breed has made this harsh environment its home. Behold, the Alaskan Malamute. This canine's roots run deep into the history and culture of the indigenous peoples of Alaska, and its presence is as indomitable as the glaciers that grace its homeland.

The Alaskan Malamute's name comes from the native Mahlemiut people, who inhabited the western part of Alaska. These dogs were integral to the Mahlemiut's way of life for centuries. These majestic canines were bred for their immense strength, endurance, and ability to haul heavy loads across long distances. The Malamute's partnership with the Mahlemiut was symbiotic, with the dogs providing invaluable assistance in hunting, transportation, and survival in the harsh Arctic environment.

As European settlers ventured into Alaska during the late 19th century and the gold rush era, they encountered these powerful dogs and quickly recognized their utility. The Alaskan Malamute played a crucial role in the exploration of Alaska, often accompanying sled teams on perilous journeys through the frozen wilderness. These dogs were essential for transporting supplies and people to remote mining camps and settlements.

Distinctive Physical Features

The Alaskan Malamute is an imposing and strikingly beautiful breed. They are large, strong dogs with a well-muscled, sturdy frame. Adorning their broad head is a distinctive "Mal" mask, which contrasts sharply with their expressive almond-shaped eyes. Their eyes can be brown or amber and exude an intelligent and friendly expression.

One of the most distinctive features of the Alaskan Malamute is their thick double coat. This coat is designed to provide insulation against the extreme cold and consists of a dense, soft undercoat and a coarse outer coat. Their coat color varies and can include shades of gray, black, sable, and red. Malamutes often have a white face mask, a white belly, legs, feet, paws, and a plume-like tail carried over their back.

Their powerful legs are well-suited for endurance, and their feet are equipped with tough, cushioned pads to handle the rugged terrain of the Arctic. The Malamute's imposing appearance reflects its strength and ability to perform heavy-duty tasks.

Temperament Traits

The Alaskan Malamute is known for its friendly and affectionate nature. They are friendly dogs that form strong bonds with their families and are often described as gentle giants. Their friendly disposition makes them excellent family pets, especially in homes with children. Malamutes are typically tolerant and patient, which can be particularly important in households with young children.

Despite their large size, Malamutes often believe they are lap dogs and enjoy being close to their human companions. Their affectionate nature also extends to strangers, as they are generally welcoming and warm with visitors. This friendly demeanor makes them poor guard dogs, but their presence alone can be a deterrent due to their size and strength.

Training Challenges and Tips

Training an Alaskan Malamute can be a rewarding but sometimes challenging endeavor. These dogs are intelligent but have an independent streak that can lead to stubbornness. Training should begin early in a Malamute's life, ideally during puppyhood, to establish boundaries and expectations.

Consistency and positive reinforcement methods are essential when training a Malamute. They respond well to rewards, praise, and treats for good behavior. Harsh training methods or punishment can be counterproductive and may lead to resistance or anxiety in the dog.

Malamutes have a strong prey drive, which means they may be inclined to chase smaller animals. This instinct should be taken into consideration when training and socializing them around other pets.

Health Concerns and Care

Alaskan Malamutes are generally healthy dogs with a life expectancy of 10 to 14 years. However, like all breeds, they can be susceptible to certain health issues. One common concern is hip dysplasia, a genetic condition that affects the hip joints and can lead to arthritis and mobility issues. Responsible breeding practices and regular veterinary check-ups can help mitigate the risk of hip dysplasia.

Another condition to watch for is bloat, a potentially life-threatening condition affecting deep-chested breeds like the Malamute. Feeding multiple smaller meals throughout the day, rather than one large meal, can help reduce the risk of bloat. Additionally, Malamutes should not engage in strenuous exercise immediately after eating.

Routine grooming is necessary to maintain the Malamute's thick coat. Regular brushing helps remove loose hair and prevent matting. Shedding seasons, which occur twice a year, may require more frequent brushing. Bathing should be done as needed, but not too frequently, to avoid drying out their skin and coat.

Famous Alaskan Malamute Expeditions and Stories

The Alaskan Malamute's history is filled with tales of adventure and bravery. One such story is Admiral Richard Byrd's 1928 expedition to Antarctica. Malamutes were chosen for the team due to their exceptional strength and endurance. They played a vital role in hauling supplies and equipment across the treacherous Antarctic terrain, contributing to the expedition's success.

In the world of cinema, the Malamute has left its mark with the iconic film "The Call of the Wild." Based on Jack London's novel, the story features a heroic Malamute named Buck, whose journey of survival and self-discovery in the Yukon wilderness has captured the imaginations of generations.

Continuing to explore the world of Arctic breeds will uncover more stories of the Alaskan Malamute's remarkable contributions to history and society. These dogs are beloved companions and heroes in their own right, embodying the enduring spirit of the Arctic wilderness.

4

Samoyed

Historical Background and Heritage

Snow and ice stretch as far as the eye can see in the heart of the Arctic. With its warm and inviting smile, the Samoyed has been a beloved companion of indigenous peoples for centuries. This breed's history is intertwined with the nomadic Samoyedic people of Siberia, who relied on these dogs for their unwavering loyalty and exceptional adaptability to the harsh Arctic conditions.

The Samoyed's origins can be traced back to the Samoyedic people, who roamed the vast tundra of Siberia for thousands of years. These nomadic tribes depended on their reindeer herds for sustenance, and the Samoyed dogs played a crucial role in herding and guarding these animals. The breed's name, Samoyed, is a tribute to these people who cherished their canine companions.

Samoyeds were not just working dogs; they were part of the family. They slept in the tents of the Samoyedic people, providing warmth during the frigid nights and companionship during the long, sunless winters. This close bond between humans and dogs forged a breed known for its friendly and gentle temperament.

Unique Appearance and Coat Characteristics

The Samoyed's appearance is as distinctive as its history. These dogs are known for their striking, fluffy white coat that seems to defy the cold and harsh Arctic climate. Their thick fur consists of two layers—a soft, insulating undercoat and a longer, coarser outer coat. This combination provides insulation against the cold, while their dense fur also helps protect them from biting insects during the summer months.

The Samoyed's coat is not only functional but also incredibly beautiful. Their dark eyes, which exude intelligence and friendliness, are framed by a distinctive black "eyeliner" that enhances their expressive faces. Their ears stand erect and they often carry their tails over their backs in a gentle curve. The Samoyed's appearance is one of grace, elegance, and charm.

Sociable Temperament and Interaction with Humans

One of the most endearing qualities of the Samoyed is its friendly and affectionate nature. They are known for their friendly disposition and love for human companionship. Samoyeds thrive on being part of a family and are known to form strong bonds with their owners.

This breed is often described as "smiling" due to their upturned lips and sparkling eyes, which give the impression of a perpetual grin. Their happy and friendly demeanor makes them excellent family pets and great companions for children. Samoyeds are typically gentle and patient, which is particularly important in households with young family members.

Due to their friendly nature, Samoyeds are generally welcoming of strangers. While they may not make the best guard dogs, their presence alone can be a deterrent due to their size and the perception of friendliness.

Training Strategies for Samoyeds

Training a Samoyed is a rewarding experience, thanks to their intelligence and eagerness to please. These dogs respond well to positive reinforcement techniques, such as praise, treats, and play. Harsh training methods or punishment are typically unnecessary and counterproductive, as Samoyeds may become uncooperative or anxious.

Early socialization is vital for Samoyeds to become well-adjusted and confident dogs. Introducing them to various people, animals, and environments from a young age can help prevent shyness or aggression. Socialization also helps curb any tendencies towards stubbornness or assertiveness.

Samoyeds are active dogs and require regular exercise to stay happy and healthy. Daily walks, playtime, and dog sports can help them burn off their energy and provide mental stimulation. Without adequate exercise, they may become bored and engage in undesirable behaviors.

Common Health Issues and Preventive Measures

Samoyeds are generally healthy dogs with a life expectancy of around 12 to 14 years. However, like all breeds, they can be susceptible to specific health issues. One of the common concerns in Samoyeds is hip dysplasia, a genetic condition that affects the hip joints and can lead to arthritis and mobility issues. Responsible breeding practices and regular veterinary check-ups can help mitigate the risk of hip dysplasia.

Another condition to watch for is progressive retinal atrophy (PRA), an inherited eye disease that can lead to vision loss. Regular eye examinations by a veterinary ophthalmologist can help monitor and manage this condition.

Samoyeds are also prone to certain skin conditions, such as hot spots and allergies. Routine grooming is essential to keep their dense coat clean and mat-free. Regular brushing can help remove loose hair and reduce shedding, which can be particularly heavy during seasonal changes.

Samoyed Involvement in Exploration and Adventure

Throughout history, Samoyeds have been steadfast companions in the world of exploration and adventure. One notable example is their involvement in polar expeditions. These dogs played a crucial role in the early 20th century when explorers braved the icy and treacherous landscapes of the North and South Poles.

In 1928, Australian explorer Sir Douglas Mawson embarked on an expedition to Antarctica accompanied by a team of Samoyeds. These dogs helped haul equipment and supplies across the harsh and unforgiving terrain, contributing to the expedition's success. The courage and resilience of these Samoyeds in the face of extreme conditions showcased the breed's remarkable capabilities.

Diving deeper into the world of Arctic breeds will uncover many more stories of the Samoyed's involvement in exploration, their enduring loyalty, and their unique place in the history of Arctic canines. These dogs are not just companions but adventurers, explorers, and cherished family members.

5

Greenland Dog

Cultural Significance and Historical Context

In the grand tapestry of Arctic canines, the Greenland Dog embodies strength, endurance, and cultural significance. With a history deeply interwoven with the Arctic's indigenous peoples, these dogs have not only been companions but vital partners in survival. As we delve into the world of the Greenland Dog, we uncover a fascinating story of resilience, loyalty, and adaptability

To understand the Greenland Dog fully, one must grasp its integral role in the culture and history of the Inuit people of Greenland. In Greenland's vast and frozen landscapes, where the elements are unforgiving and the climate severe, the Greenland Dog has been a steadfast companion and indispensable tool for survival.

The Inuit people, who have inhabited the Arctic regions of Greenland for centuries, have relied upon the Greenland Dog for their very existence. These dogs played multifaceted roles in Inuit life, from hunting partners to sled pullers. Their contributions extended to hunting seals, polar bears, and other wildlife, providing vital sustenance to Inuit communities. In essence, the Greenland Dog was not just a working animal but a lifeline.

But beyond utility, the Greenland Dog held a special place in the hearts of the Inuit. Their loyalty and companionship transcended their roles as mere helpers. In Inuit households, these dogs were considered family, their presence providing warmth and solace in the harshest of climates.

Robust Physical Build and Adaptations

The physical characteristics of the Greenland Dog mirror their capacity to thrive in the extreme Arctic environment. These dogs are built solid, exhibiting remarkable strength and endurance. Their physique is medium to large, ideally suited for the demands of Arctic life.

A defining feature of the Greenland Dog is its double coat, consisting of a dense undercoat and a coarser outer coat. This natural insulation protects them from the biting cold and blustering winds sweeping Greenland's tundra and fjords. Among their distinctive features, their erect, triangular ears stand out, a testament to their adaptation for withstanding frostbite. Their tails, bushy and often curled over their backs, further insulate their hindquarters.

With sturdy legs and well-padded feet, Greenland Dogs are equipped to navigate the rugged and challenging terrain of the Arctic. Their physical attributes make them adept at pulling sleds through snow and ice, a task central to their historical role.

Independent Yet Loyal Temperament

The Greenland Dog possesses a temperament that blends independence with loyalty, a balance honed through generations of surviving in a harsh environment. Their independent nature enables them to make decisions when human guidance is lacking, a valuable trait in the unforgiving Arctic wilderness.

Yet, this independence does not diminish their loyalty and attachment to their human families. Greenland Dogs form strong bonds with their owners, often demonstrating affection and protectiveness. Inuit households consider them as working partners and cherished companions, offering solace and warmth on cold Arctic nights.

Resilience and adaptability are hallmarks of the Greenland Dog's temperament. They are known for their ability to endure extreme cold, traverse challenging terrain, and work tirelessly—a testament to their indispensability in Inuit life.

Training Considerations for Greenland Dogs

Training a Greenland Dog requires understanding their independent nature and historical self-reliance. These dogs are intelligent and resourceful but can also be strong-willed. Practical training methods involve patience, consistency, and positive reinforcement.

Early socialization is crucial to ensure Greenland Dogs are well-adjusted and comfortable in various situations. Exposure to different people, animals, and environments from a young age can help prevent shyness or fearfulness.

Given their hunting instincts, Greenland Dogs may have a strong prey drive. It's essential to supervise them around smaller animals. Recall training is critically important, as their independent nature may lead them to wander if inadequately trained.

Health Factors and Care Guidelines

Greenland Dogs are generally robust and healthy, with a life expectancy of 10 to 13 years. However, like all breeds, they may be susceptible to certain health issues. One common concern is hip dysplasia, a genetic condition that affects the hip joints and can lead to arthritis and mobility issues. Responsible breeding practices and regular veterinary check-ups can help mitigate the risk of hip dysplasia.

In the harsh Arctic environment, frostbite and hypothermia can harm Greenland Dogs. Proper shelter and care during extreme weather conditions are essential to prevent these issues.

Routine grooming is necessary to maintain the Greenland Dog's coat and prevent matting. Regular brushing helps remove loose hair and keeps their fur clean. They may require more frequent brushing during shedding seasons.

Greenland Dogs in Polar Exploration and Traditional Use

Throughout history, Greenland Dogs have played a pivotal role in polar exploration and traditional Inuit life. These dogs were essential to the success of explorers who ventured into the frozen Arctic and Antarctic expanses.

In 1911, Norwegian explorer Roald Amundsen achieved a historic milestone by reaching the South Pole, and Greenland Dogs played a vital part in the expedition. These dogs endured extreme conditions and hauled supplies across the vast and unforgiving Antarctic terrain.

In addition to exploration, Greenland Dogs continue to play vital roles in the lives of the Inuit people. Their significance in traditional Inuit life underscores their enduring importance and resilience in the Arctic.

Further exploration into Arctic canines will reveal the Greenland Dog as a symbol of cultural heritage, resilience, and the enduring bond between humans and their loyal companions in the harshest environments.

6

Canadian Eskimo Dog

Indigenous Heritage and Traditional Roles

In the realm of Arctic canines, the Canadian Eskimo Dog stands as a testament to the enduring legacy of indigenous peoples and their canine companions in the harshest of environments. This breed embodies the spirit of the North, with its rich heritage deeply rooted in the traditional life of the Arctic's indigenous inhabitants.

The Canadian Eskimo Dog, also known as the Qimmiq, holds a special place in the hearts of Canada's indigenous peoples, notably the Inuit and other Northern communities. This breed has been a vital part of their traditional way of life for centuries, fulfilling many roles beyond mere companionship.

In the frigid landscapes of the Canadian Arctic, where temperatures can plummet to bone-chilling lows, Canadian Eskimo Dogs were essential to the survival of indigenous communities. They were reliable hunting partners, assisting in the pursuit of seals, polar bears, and other wildlife that provided sustenance to these communities. Their strength and endurance made them indispensable in transporting people and supplies and pulling sleds across vast, snowy expanses.

Beyond their practical roles, Canadian Eskimo Dogs were revered as family members. They provided warmth and companionship in the isolation of the Arctic, forging deep bonds with their human counterparts.

Physical Features and Adaptations

The Canadian Eskimo Dog's physical features reflect its ability to thrive in the unforgiving Arctic landscape. These dogs are medium to large, with strong, muscular bodies built for endurance. Their double coat, consisting of a dense undercoat and a protective outer layer, shields them from the extreme cold.

One of the most striking features of the Canadian Eskimo Dog is its wolf-like appearance. With erect ears, a thick mane of fur around the neck, and a bushy tail, they exude an air of wild elegance. Their almond-shaped eyes are alert and intelligent, reflecting their keen awareness of their surroundings.

Their powerful legs and large, well-padded feet are perfectly adapted for navigating the snowy terrain of the Arctic. These physical attributes make them exceptional sled dogs, capable of hauling heavy loads across long distances.

Strong-willed yet Gentle Temperament

The Canadian Eskimo Dog possesses a unique temperament characterized by a blend of strength, independence, and gentleness. They are renowned for their loyalty and dedication to their families, making them excellent companions for those who understand their needs.

Despite their strong-willed nature, Canadian Eskimo Dogs are known for their gentleness and patience, especially with children. They are generally friendly and sociable, making them suitable for family life.

However, their independent streak may require experienced handling and training. Early socialization is crucial to ensure they are well-adjusted and comfortable in various situations.

Training Challenges and Success Stories

Training a Canadian Eskimo Dog can be a rewarding but challenging endeavor. Their independent nature and strong-willed disposition require patience, consistency, and positive reinforcement techniques. Early socialization is essential to prevent behavioral issues.

One of the most remarkable aspects of Canadian Eskimo Dogs is their adaptability and intelligence. They excel in a wide range of activities, from obedience and agility trials to weight-pulling competitions. Their quick learning ability and natural athleticism make them exceptional working dogs.

The success stories of Canadian Eskimo Dogs in various dog sports and competitions testify to their potential when provided with the proper training and stimulation. These dogs thrive when engaged in physical and mental challenges, showcasing their versatility and resilience.

Health Considerations and Preventive Care

Canadian Eskimo Dogs are generally healthy and hardy, with a lifespan of around 12 to 15 years. However, like all breeds, they may be susceptible to specific health issues.

One common concern is hip dysplasia, a genetic condition that affects the hip joints and can lead to mobility issues and pain. Responsible breeding practices, including hip evaluations, can help reduce the risk of this condition.

Regular veterinary check-ups are essential to monitor the overall health of Canadian Eskimo Dogs. Dental care is also critical, as they can be prone to dental problems.

Canadian Eskimo Dogs in Modern Times

While the traditional way of life in the Arctic has evolved, the Canadian Eskimo Dog's significance endures. In modern times, these dogs continue to play roles in various capacities, from working dogs in remote communities to cherished family pets.

Efforts are underway to preserve and protect this unique breed, which faces challenges due to its small population. Organizations dedicated to the breed's preservation are working to ensure its continued existence, recognizing the importance of the Canadian Eskimo Dog as a symbol of Canada's Northern heritage.

Upon further examination into the world of Arctic canines, the Canadian Eskimo Dog emerges as a living embodiment of the North's enduring spirit. Their heritage, adaptability, and loyalty are a testament to the bond between humans and their faithful companions in the face of adversity.

7

Conclusion

As we conclude our comprehensive journey into the captivating world of Arctic canines, it is essential to reflect on the wealth of knowledge we have uncovered about these remarkable breeds. From the regal Siberian Husky to the indomitable Canadian Eskimo Dog, these five majestic breeds have given us a glimpse into the Arctic's enduring spirit and the extraordinary bond between humans and their faithful companions.

Summarizing Key Points

Throughout our exploration, we have delved deep into the historical origins, physical characteristics, temperamental traits, training challenges, health considerations, and remarkable achievements of each breed. We have witnessed the Siberian Husky's boundless energy and the Alaskan Malamute's unwavering loyalty. We marveled at the Samoyed's unique appearance and the Greenland Dog's independent yet loyal temperament. Finally, we celebrated the Canadian Eskimo Dog's strong-willed nature and gentle disposition.

Through these chapters, we have gained a comprehensive understanding of what makes Arctic breeds unique and why they have captured the hearts of those who have had the privilege of knowing them.

Emphasizing the Importance of Responsible Ownership

While these breeds are undeniably captivating and resilient, it is vital to remember that they are not just pets but a commitment. Responsible ownership of Arctic canines requires dedication, patience, and a deep understanding of their distinct needs. From providing adequate exercise and mental stimulation to ensuring their health and well-being, the responsibility of caring for these dogs should not be underestimated.

We have learned that proper training and socialization are crucial for Arctic breeds to thrive in a modern environment. Their innate traits and independent spirits demand thoughtful handling and consistent positive reinforcement.

Encouraging Preservation of Arctic Breeds

The heritage of these Arctic canines is a living testament to the history and traditions of the North. As we move forward, we are responsible for protecting these breeds, ensuring that they continue to grace our world with their presence.

Breed organizations and enthusiasts safeguard the future of these Arctic canines. By supporting these initiatives and promoting responsible breeding practices, we can contribute to the long-term well-being of these magnificent dogs.

Looking Towards the Future of Arctic Canines

The future of Arctic canines is intertwined with our own. As we venture into an ever-changing world, we must carry forward the lessons learned from these resilient and devoted companions. Their adaptability, loyalty, and strength in the face of adversity serve as an inspiration to us all.

Whether it is the enduring spirit of exploration, the unwavering commitment to their human families, or their ability to thrive in the harshest of environments, Arctic canines have left an indelible mark on our hearts and in our history.

As we conclude this journey through the Arctic wilderness, may we always remember the lessons these breeds have taught us. Let us carry forward their legacy with respect, love, and a deep appreciation for the extraordinary connection between humans and their Arctic companions.

We appreciate your interest in our book. If you enjoyed it, please leave us a review!

Resources

Open AI. (2024). ChatGPT (GPT-4) [Software]. Open AI. https://www.openai.com/

Open AI. (2024). DALL-E [Software]. Open AI. https://www.openai.com/

www.ingramcontent.com/pod-product-compliance
Lightning Source LLC
Chambersburg PA
CBHW061936270726
48660CB00007BA/2934